Journal of Tears

What one woman experienced and learned in God's school of suffering due to broken marriage vows.

by Elizabeth Lapp

Introduction: Simon Schrock
Cover Photo: Noah Petersheim

ISBN: 0-87813-522-7

Dedication

To my two dear, young daughters, Marilyn and Beverly, who contributed their childlike faith and love during the long months of heartache and disappointment. And to my very young son, Jason, whose sunny personality was a shining light as I found the way through the valley.

Acknowledgments

I am deeply grateful . . .

To God for His leading;

To my niece, Frieda Stoltzfus, for suggesting that I write;

To my friends, Diane Drumeler and Dorothy Rechenberg, for typing the manuscript;

And to David and Pauline Harrison and Dora Taylor for their assistance in proofreading and editing.

Introduction

Truly remarkable! In the midst of an "adulterous and sinful generation," here is a testimony of living by the principles of what is right over what is popular opinion of the day.

How do you live in a world that ignores vows and commitments like the latest political promise? How does one keep faith and sanity in a world where divorce and breaking promises is accepted as the norm? How do you remain faithful to your God and an unfaithful partner?

Finding such a person in today's society stands out like a bright rose in a thorn bush. It is truly beautiful and encouraging to meet one who chose another way from the routine easy escape solutions of our day. Elizabeth Lapp's response to trials and testing of an unfaithful husband is indeed refreshing.

Read on and feel her deep hurts and frustrations, along with the painful path of choosing her responses and reactions on the basis of what is Scripturally right.

Enter into her "caved-in" world, the path of suffering, conflicting advice, the choosing to forgive, and the patience of hanging on while it was painfully difficult. Exercise the pain reliever of faith, commitment, prayer, and hope. Walk with her through dark moments when the grace of God was there to gently grant victory and deliverance.

To keep a vow until death for Elizabeth Lapp has been painful. To have kept that vow is a most commendable example to this generation.

I recommend this book to anyone, and especially those who are hurting and struggling in their commitments.

My admiration goes to the author for her faithfulness and vision in seeing that the best is yet to come!

You will be enriched by exploring these pages.

Simon Schrock
April, 1984

Preface

April 16, 1966, was the day of our wedding. By evening my cheeks were sore from smiling. I was so happy! I little dreamed our marriage would end as a divorce statistic. But because it has, and because this is happening to many others, I was inspired to write the following pages. I have found that God's Word has the answer and that God Himself is the answer to our deepest needs.

When my husband became unfaithful, my world was completely shattered. In the past five years I have picked up the broken pieces of my life and journeyed from brokenness to healing. It has been a long journey, groping for answers, making decisions, working through rejection, loneliness, shattered hopes, and much more.

If you are hurting, if words such as *suffering, pain, affliction,* and *tears* are words you relate to, I hope the following pages will help you to wholeness and healing. Because God has helped me through my heartaches, I desire to help you through yours. As that happens, God is being glorified and it adds meaning and purpose to my experience, unpleasant as it has been.

Contents

Chapter 1

When My World Caved In

"Many are the afflictions of the righteous" (Psalm 34:19).

The following letter was written out of desperation to my husband several months after I learned the soul-shattering news that I was no longer the only woman in his life. We could not communicate as before because of a gigantic wall that had arisen between us; therefore, I resorted to letter writing, something I still find myself doing two and one-half years later because verbal communication seems impossible.

Dear Husband,

Please bear with me as I write to you. Somehow we do not seem to get anywhere by talking, so I shall resort to writing.

This past week has been one of severe torment for me. My mind is filled with fear and doubt and distrust and hopelessness. I do not want to live any longer. Satan has been hurling overwhelming temptations at me. One night I read the Bible and prayed until one o'clock trying to find victory and peace. When I went to bed, I had a fitful night of sleep, full of bad dreams. I fear for our unborn baby if I do not find peace of mind. Our marriage is a wreck; soon it will be destroyed at the rate we are going. Since we cannot discuss it, we need to go to a counselor. We need help to put our marriage back together, and we need help now. It is very dangerous for me and the baby to go through more weeks like this one. If we would be physically ill we would see a doctor, and it is just as necessary when we are spiritually ill.

We are completely missing what God has for us. Remember back over the past eleven years. There was love, laughter, sharing, affection, togetherness, understanding, care, and praise. I was the one and only in your life. Remember our first night together, how we knelt by our bed and dedicated our lives and marriage to God. Remember our extreme joy at the birth of our first daughter and four years later our second one. We desired to give them the best Christian home to grow up in. It breaks my heart to have our marriage crumble. Could we, will we, seek help?

Desperate,
Your Wife

Chapter 2

Why, God, Why?

"No chastening for the present seemeth to be joyous" (Hebrews 12:11).

When calamity strikes, the one question that rises like a monster is, "Why, God, why?" I knew that I was not to question God. I knew He loved me and knew what was best for me and would not test me beyond my strength. I knew He was the Blessed Controller of all things. However, all that did not erase the question, "Why?"

As a teenager, I was more hesitant about marriage than most girls seem to be. I realized that many marriages are not happy. During my courtship years I prayed, "Lord, do not allow me to get married if mine cannot be a happy Christian home." So I wondered, "Why this, Lord?" I sought God's will in marriage, yet as I looked around at others who probably did not, they seemed to be getting along fine. Why? I never committed any gross sins in my life, but I wondered whether I was reaping or being chastened.

I realized as a wife I had faults and failures and I wondered if I had brought this upon myself. Still, I asked, "Why *me,* Lord?" I could think of home situations where wives did not love or appreciate their husbands. Why didn't it happen to them? Why me? I was tempted to think God's dealing with me was very harsh. I felt I must be terrible for God to have to deal with me like this. Others did not seem to be suffering as I was. Why me? I felt my motives, ideals, and dreams concerning marriage were pure and God-honoring. Why me, Lord?

Someone told me God must have planned this situation, then looked down from heaven and chose to give it to me knowing I would be able to handle it without losing my faith in Him. Was that why?

The daily devotional booklet I was reading said, "When God allows tremendous trials in our lives, it is because we are special. He has confidence in our ability to handle it." Did God have that kind of confidence in me?

Somewhere I learned that God needs people to display His grace. Was I to be a model of God's grace? But why me?

Someone else said, "The Lord allows distressing situations to come into our lives to teach us to walk closer to Him." But I loved the Lord and thought I was walking close to Him. I was living for Him the best I knew how. So, why me?

For months I read every book I could find on the subject of suffering. The following are some of the thoughts I gleaned: Jesus also faced loneliness, betrayal of friends, rejection, and disappointment. He knows my problems through and through. I am not alone. Other Christians have faced similar problems and have come through. Because I have Christ, I do not need to cave in under life's problems. I must stand, pick up the Bible, feed upon its strengthening verses, throw aside self-pity, and cast myself wholly on God's promises. God is faithful. There is hope. God never sends trials heavier than I can bear. The intensity with which they come, and the point in life at which we must face them are all tailor-made by God. No trials hang too long on us. They fit precisely. I will have strength for today only, not tomorrow. Every trial will come to an end; every problem has a solution. No matter how dark the night, the morning will come.

Over and over I read the Book of I Peter. He seemed to have the most to say about suffering. Sometimes in the middle

of the night I would try to comfort myself
as I read the words:

"Wherein ye greatly rejoice,
though now for a season, if need be,
ye are in heaviness through manifold
temptations" (I Peter 1:6).

"For what glory is it, if, when ye be
buffeted for your faults, ye shall take
it patiently? but if, when ye do well,
and suffer for it, ye take it patiently,
this is acceptable with God. For even
hereunto were ye called: because
Christ also suffered for us, leaving us
an example, that ye should follow his
steps" (I Peter 2:20, 21).

"The eyes of the Lord are over the
righteous, and his ears are open unto
their prayers" (I Peter 3:12).

"It is better, if the will of God be so,
that ye suffer for well doing, than for
evil doing. For Christ also hath once
suffered" (I Peter 3:17, 18).

"Beloved, think it not strange concerning the fiery trial which is to try
you . . . but rejoice . . . that, when his
glory shall be revealed, ye may be

glad also with exceeding joy" (I Peter 4:12, 13).

"Wherefore let them that suffer according to the will of God commit the keeping of their souls to him in well doing, as unto a faithful Creator" (I Peter 4:19).

"Whom resist [Satan] steadfast in the faith, knowing that the same afflictions are accomplished in your brethren that are in the world. But the God of all grace, who hath called us unto his eternal glory by Christ Jesus, after that ye have suffered a while, make you perfect, stablish, strengthen, settle you" (I Peter 5:9, 10).

As I saturated my mind with these words, I could visualize a future glory. At other times I felt like screaming, "Forget the future glory, Lord. All I want is to be happy now." When I read James 1:2 where it says, "Count it all joy when ye fall into divers temptations," I wanted to say, "Be happy about difficulties? Why? It hurts too much to be happy. How can I be happy when I hurt?"

However, today as I view suffering, I realize it is only as I view it in the light of eternity and the future glory that I can faithfully endure unto the end. Only as I completely believe that God's Word is true can I rejoice and be happy in spite of tremendous trials. "The sufferings of this present time are not worthy to be compared with the glory which shall be revealed in us" (Romans 8:18).

Chapter 3

Grace and Humility

"God resisteth the proud, but giveth grace unto the humble" (James 4:6).

One evening my husband announced that he was not going to go to church with me any longer. He said, "The church is full of hypocrites, and I am getting out of the bubble." I was shattered to the very depth of my inner being. I asked him if I should give it up too, and he said, "Not if it means something to you."

When Sunday morning came, he was not home. I thought I could not go to church alone, but I did not know how I would explain to my children. It was the most humiliating thing I ever had to do. When I walked into church alone, I felt like I was wearing a sign that said, "I have problems."

The first several Sundays I went alone, I left a little before the service was over to avoid being seen and to avoid talking to people because I was nothing but a bucketful of tears. But I could not play games forever. I felt like I was stripped of every ounce of pride as I opened myself to people and shared that I had a problem much bigger than I could handle.

As I humbled myself before God and man by being open and honest, God's grace began pouring into my life. People were extremely kind and thoughtful. The most precious words to my breaking heart were, "I am praying for you." I could not believe the people, and the number of people, that were saying it to me. I felt so unworthy of all the love that

20

was being shown to me.

Grace is God's divine enablement for living and I knew His Word said that it would be sufficient. I began each day asking God for grace to sustain me. I knew within myself I did not have what it took. I learned that grace was available but that I had to appropriate it. If I asked God for grace for the day, I had to appropriate it by getting out of bed and beginning my day. I learned that grace does not take the pain of a broken heart away, but it makes it bearable.

Chapter 4

Guidance

"My sheep hear my voice" (John 10:27).

Many times when a person is afflicted with an incurable illness, he will run from one physician to another hoping to find a cure or a remedy.

This is how I was at the beginning of my affliction. I told my story to everyone who would listen, hoping someone would have a sure cure for my marriage situation.

Along with sharing my situation with everyone that would listen came bushels of advice. I found myself struggling to know what voices to heed. How could I know what God really wanted me to do?

In response to my husband's actions, some people were sure that love was the answer. The advice was to keep the door of reconciliation open and never, never close it. Continue to love and submit and wait patiently; surely God will do a work in his life.

Others were sure I did not need to put up with this. They suggested to give him the "either straighten up or else" treatment.

Both lines of advice were coming from Christian people. How was I to know which voices to listen to?

Along with deciding how to respond to my husband were a multitude of other decisions to make. I could not turn to my husband for advice, so naturally I turned to other people, and again I often received conflicting advice. All this left me quite frustrated when decisions had to be

23

made.

One night I cried out to God in desperation saying, "Lord, help me, I cannot make all these decisions—the responsibility is too great." As usual, when I became desperate, God gave me an answer.

God showed me that I must put myself under the authority of another. God provided the husband to be in authority over his wife. When the umbrella of protection is removed by death or separation, the woman is to place herself under another authority. It could be a father or father-in-law or a pastor or elder in the church. She then can receive advice and direction through the authority over her. This revelation gave me new freedom and protection.

As I studied further, God showed me four other ways to discern His leading:

First, through His Word. We should never expect a separate, direct, personal revelation on something God has already stated in His Word. When God's Word tells us to do something, we ought to

24

obey. If we ignore His Word and look for special revelations, we open ourselves to delusion and error.

Second, God leads us through circumstances. He uses open and closed doors, and we never need to force doors open. If something is His will, He will clear the way for us.

Third, God leads through our own good judgment or common sense. "God hath not given us the spirit of fear; but . . . of a sound mind" (II Timothy 1:7).

Fourth, God leads through the Holy Spirit's promptings within. He gives us an inner urge or desire.

The suggestions of those in authority over us, Scripture, circumstances, common sense, and the Holy Spirit's prompting—all five should harmonize before we move forward. I learned that with right decisions God also gives a peace within.

One particularly big decision I had to make found me in conflict with the one under whose authority I had placed myself. I struggled and struggled with no peace until I yielded to his advice, and then I was flooded with peace. It would have been a serious mistake had I taken my way.

When I fail to follow or when I misinterpret God's guidance, I trust and pray that He will work in spite of my wrong decisions. He is big enough to do that.

In Isaiah, Jesus is called the Counselor. I am learning to know Him as such. Today I no longer need to share with everyone. The voices are not as many. With God, my authority, my pastor, and the Bible, I am enabled to make decisions and find God's will in my answers. God is good! Glory to His name!

Chapter 5

Prayer

"Ask, and it shall be given you" (Matthew 7:7).

I wanted desperately for my husband to come back to God and back to me and my family. But prayers did not seem to be heard. I was praying. Friends, families, and whole churches were praying, but nothing happened. Months went by and there was no evidence that God was working.

One day I wrote in my diary, "Lord, how long must we rend the heavens with our prayers?" I was asking everyone, "Why doesn't God answer our prayers?" I received many answers. They said things such as, "Did you try thanking God for the situation just as it is?"

One lady shared a difficult situation and said when she began thanking God, He performed a miracle. So I prayed thank-you prayers.

Another would say, "Stop begging God; just commit the whole thing to Him once and for all and leave it there." So I endeavored to do that.

Another said, "God doesn't answer selfish prayers. You cannot ask God to bring your husband back to you; just pray that he would come back to God." So I searched my life for selfish motives and pleaded with God for my husband's salvation.

Another said, "The Bible says, 'Bless them that curse you.' Pray blessing on your husband. Ask God every day to bless him financially, physically, and spiritually. One woman began praying blessing upon her non-Christian husband and soon he became saved." Well, praying that was not difficult. I figured if God would bless him in all those ways, I would get some of the benefits, too.

Then another would say, "Maybe if we would pray that God would make him miserable, he would repent." I knew the Bible says, "The way of transgressors is hard" and, "There is no peace . . . to the wicked." It seemed logical that if we would ask God to make these verses a reality in his life, the misery of it all might cause him to repent.

Others said, "We can pray, but remember, God does not work against a person's will. He has a will, and God will never force him." I was of the belief that God can bring circumstances into a person's life to make him willing, so that was not going to keep me from praying. Why else did God put Jonah in the whale's belly but to make him willing?

Others thought the more we pray the more power, so we had several group-size prayer meetings.

Another said, "God will answer our prayers. It is just that God's time is not our time."

All of this left me sometimes confused about prayer.

But throughout, I was and continue to be deeply touched by the prayers of my own children. Surely a child's prayer is not selfish or out of a wrong motive or out of unbelief. How can God turn a deaf ear when a five-year-old prays, "Dear God, we want Daddy to come back and be our daddy; we really do. Help his girlfriend to get a Christian. Thank You that I have a mommy that stays with me. Just help Daddy to walk with Jesus again. Amen."

I still have questions about prayer, but I am content to pray every day that God will work in my husband's life in whatever time and way is necessary to bring him back to Jesus. My petition is that God would continue to convict him, draw him, and speak to him every day. I believe if we ask anything according to His will, He hears us. I believe my faith in

God needs to remain firm and fixed regardless of His response to my prayers.

Trust God Patiently

Although I've asked God every day,
   These many anxious years,
And yet the blessing has not come,
   I still believe He hears!

I know that He does answer prayers
   Sometimes unseen to man,
Then I shall trust and wait 'till I
   Can see God's deeper plan.

Perhaps the things for which I prayed
   Were not the best for me,
But 'till I know, I'll importune
   And trust God patiently.
                    —F. M. Bates

Chapter 6

To Live or Die

"If thou faint in the day of adversity, thy strength is small" (Proverbs 24:10).

To live or die is not a choice God planned for us to make. However, when life becomes too painful, one may be faced with the temptation to end it, thinking death could not be worse. One day I wrote in my diary:

"I'm depressed. The only way out of this situation is death. This tor-

32

ture may continue for years, and I'm tired of it. I cannot stand it any longer. It is torture to know your husband is giving his time and attention and love to another. The only thing that has kept me going the last eighteen months is prayer, God's Word, constant discipline of the mind, and hope. I'm tired of praying and meditating and disciplining my mind, and there seems to be no hope. Everyone is saying, 'Hang in there.' Well, I'm tired of hanging in there. The Bible says, 'Hope deferred maketh the heart sick' (Proverbs 13:12). And my heart is sick."

When a woman is married, much of her life revolves around her husband. You only realize how much when for some reason he is not there anymore.

Does a woman have a reason to live if she cannot live for her husband? I was face to face with this decision. I decided Paul's motto must become mine. "For to me to live is Christ." Christ wants me to live for His sake. He has a work for me to do. I have three children to raise for Him. I have friends and neighbors and relatives He wants me to minister to.

The hurt remains, but I choose to live.

Chapter 7

Commitment

"Commit thy way unto the Lord" (Psalm 37:5).

As I shared with others what had happened in my life, time and again I was asked, "Have you committed it to the Lord?" Time and again I thought I was at the end of myself and I would pray the prayer of committal. But a few hours or a day or a week later I would again become extremely burdened and bogged down and would wonder if I really had committed it to the Lord, and to make sure, I would pray the prayer of committal again.

I failed to understand two things: First, that commitment is a once-and-for-all thing. When I committed myself and my husband to God, God took it. When doubts and fears arose, I did not need to commit it to God again; I only needed to reaffirm that commitment by praying, "Lord, I have given myself and my husband to You. I reaffirm that commitment right now." I would reaffirm that commitment to God as often as doubts and fears arose and rest assured that God was keeping what I had committed to Him. The reaffirming was not to remind God but rather myself that the commitment had been made.

The second thing I had to realize was that the commitment was to God. I saw commitment as taking my hands off my husband and committing him into someone else's hands, but I failed to see who the Someone else was. Not until I saw that I was putting him into God's hands did I have peace. Satan did not want me to see this because he knew God was limited as long as I did not take my hands off.

I like one person's paraphrase of Psalm 37:5: "Commit thy way unto the Lord, trust also in Him and He worketh."

I have committed myself and my husband to God, and I am trusting Him to work in the way that brings the most glory to His name.

Chapter 8

Victory

"This is the victory that overcometh
. . . even our faith" (I John 5:4).

During my time of trial, I could live
above the circumstances and feel happy
and hopeful for maybe a month at a time.
But then I would experience a day or
several days of real discouragement. Circumstances would look so hopeless. I
would cry and want to give up. On one of
those dark days I wrote the following

letter to someone:

"As time goes on and there is no change in my circumstances, I feel like I am coming apart. I know I wear a smile among people and appear to be holding up, but inside it is destroying me. For nearly two years people have been saying, 'Hang in there,' and I really feel like I am hanging. Sometimes I experience victory for awhile, but then I go down again. And my downs lately have been so low I don't know sometimes whether I'll come up again. I do my work mechanically and everything is a chore, and I'm always tired. I go through the motion of life for my children but even that is not reason enough. When my husband doesn't call me, I worry and get nervous, fearing he may never call again. When he does call, there is such a lack of communication I wish he would never call again. In the past I received a lot of help from my friends just by calling them and asking them to pray for me. But I hesitate anymore because it seems to me surely they are tired of it by now. And I feel I'll have to learn to stand on my own two feet sometime. When people say to me, 'Hang in there,' I feel as though they are just telling me to suffer on. Is it possible to live in my circumstances and not hurt? Is there a secret I have not found? I want desperately to experience victory."

This was the torrent of feeling on a down day.

I began to ask people if this was normal. Is there anything like victory every day of our lives—no blue days, no discouragements, no depression? I had experienced enough victory to know it is possible sometimes, but I wanted it all the time. I read books on the victorious life and it sounded so simple. I prayed, asking God to take away the "blue days."

I had a friend in a similar situation. She seemed to have victory all the time, until one day I caught her "down in the dumps." I began to think maybe I was normal after all. In fact, I felt a bit more free with her after that because I saw she was made of the same stuff I was. Then I began to wonder how people would relate to me if they felt I was always "on top of the world." Could God be allowing me some down days so I could relate to other human beings and so they could relate to me?

In studying the book *How to Live the Victorious Life,* by an unknown author, I learned that the victorious life is a life surrendered to Jesus Christ with Him having complete control. It is a life with all known sin confessed and forsaken. Victory is not attained once and for all; it is trusting Christ moment by moment, walking in the Spirit.

I came to realize that because I have a sin nature there are times when I do not walk in the Spirit. I also realized that because I am human, certain things in life affect my moods and may cause me to feel blue. I also had to learn to distinguish between my feelings and my will. Because I feel sad or gloomy does not mean I will be that way, and God sees my will. I learned that great truth when I studied the life of Sarah. When God told Abraham that Sarah was to have a baby, Sarah laughed and said, "Can an old woman like me have a baby?" Being human she experienced feeling and unbelief. But in Hebrews 11:11, she is recognized for her faith. Laughing was Sarah's feeling, but underneath God recognized her will to believe.

I also began to view my whole life as an aim at the ultimate victory. I consider the ultimate victory to be not losing one's faith in God but enduring until the end. I'm allowing myself some blue days without condemning myself because I believe God looks past my feelings and sees that the desire of my heart is to please Him. I continue to aim at the ultimate victory so I can say with Paul, "I have kept the faith."

Chapter 9

Love Your Enemies

"Pray for them which despitefully use you" (Matthew 5:44).

The day came when I had to tell my children the meaning of all my tears. My one daughter cried and cried as though the floodgates had opened up. My other daughter became very angry, and hateful words came pouring out of her mouth. I tried to comfort them as best I could. They still had a love for Daddy, but they hated his girlfriend. They wished she would get sick and die. They hoped she would get killed in an accident. They wished all kinds of evil upon her, and I hardly knew how to handle it. But it was no time to preach a sermon on loving your enemies, because down deep inside I had some of the same feelings. As time went on and the poison of hate that was inside had been poured out, I tried to explain to them that God is the blessed Controller of all things. He will not give us more than we can bear; we must love our enemies and realize the value of their souls. I struggled through my own feelings.

Today she is in our prayers every day. We sent her a book, telling her she is special, that God loves her, and that He has a plan for her life. We know she, too, needs Jesus and we hope sometime she will find Him. No, we have not arrived. We are glad she lives far away and we are glad we do not see her. She has played a part in bringing much grief into our lives. It takes divine love to forgive her and pray for her. Our flesh wants to seek revenge. But we are reminded, "Vengeance is mine; I will repay saith the Lord." We have put her into God's hands.

Chapter 10
Rejection

"Rejected of men, a man of sorrows and acquainted with grief" (Isaiah 53:3).

Rejection hurts. It rips at the very depth of your inner being. Only those who have experienced emotional pain know what it is. The feeling cannot be explained with words. When we experience physical pain we can go to a doctor and get medication to dull or take away the pain and discomfort. But emotional pain cannot be dulled with a pill. I learned the only way to be relieved of emotional pain is to go to the Great Physician and pour out my soul in prayer and then saturate my mind with the promises of His Word. I also found it helps to find a friend who cares and share with her. Much emotional healing took place in my life as I shared with friends who listened and cared. Counselors say that during a counseling session 75 percent of their time is spent listening, and when people get up to leave, they say, "Thank you for helping me. You did so much for me." Many times I wanted someone just to listen. I was not asking for advice.

I had to be the one to listen to my children so they could experience emotional healing also. One time my daughter said, "Mommy, it is not fun to be a little girl when Daddy does not love Mommy." My emotional pain was tripled when I saw my innocent children hurting also. I had to claim God's grace for them as well as for myself and help them appropriate it.

One day when I was feeling rejection keenly, I remembered Jesus, too, was rejected, and I cried out to Him, "Lord what did You do when people rejected You?" He seemed to say, "I gave My love to those who would accept it." And then I remembered I had three children who had not rejected me, plus many friends. I would pour my love upon them.

Rejection causes hurt. The human response to rejection is bitterness, resentment, and suchlike wrong actions.

Usually, maybe always, when one person rejects another person, it is because he has been rejected by someone and is reacting to that rejection.

Realizing what causes that behavior makes it easier to forgive. Forgiveness is the only thing that will take away the hurt of being rejected.

Having my own husband reject me has been a very deep hurt, but I am better able to respond properly to that rejection when I understand it may be caused by a deep rejection he has encountered in his life. When I am rejected, my human response would be to shut the door, but godly love holds the door open—which really is opening myself to more hurt. And only God's grace makes forgiveness and unconditional love possible.

God is not as concerned about what happens to us as about our reaction to it. Neither is He unmindful of all He has allowed to touch us.

When I respond to rejection in a godly manner, I become a demonstration of God's love.

Chapter 11

Love Never Faileth

"Charity suffereth long" (I Corinthians 13:4).

Can a woman keep on loving when her husband breaks that sacred vow which they have made, " . . . keeping yourself only for her until death do you part"? Can a woman keep on loving when her love is not returned, when she is rejected, ignored, wounded?

One day, after another crushing blow, I

sat down and cried and cried saying, "Lord, all my love for my husband has just drained out of me. I hate him; every fiber of my being wants to seek revenge. I do not want to speak to him. I do not want to see him ever again. Living without him could never be worse than living with him like this. He is only taking advantage of me. I hate him. I hate life. I am not willing to suffer anymore. He resists You and all the admonition that people have given him. He is stubborn and wicked and full of sin, and he loves it. Give him what he deserves."

After this outburst of feelings, a still, small voice within kept saying, "Charity never fails . . . bears all things . . . endures all things . . . hopes all things . . . charity never fails . . . charity never fails . . . charity never fails."

I was almost overcome by this feeling of hatred. Then I prayed, "Lord, if I am to love my husband even in all this, You will have to do it for me. I cannot, and right now I do not even want to, but cleanse me and give me Your love."

I came to realize I may not look at what my husband is now, but at what he was and what he will be. Then, by God's grace, I can still love him. I believe this is how God looked at me before I was a Christian. He saw what I could be and loved me in spite of what I was.

The love that never fails is divine. If I would say I no longer love my husband, it would be because the love I had for him was merely human. God wants me to love with divine love, and that love never fails. God can command me to love because He knows love is an act of the will. I choose to still love my husband.

Chapter 12

Forgiveness

"Forgive, if ye have ought against any" (Mark 11:25).

If my husband came to me with a repentant heart, I was quite certain I could forgive him. But one day I realized even if he did not come to ask my forgiveness, I must still forgive him. I began to see there are only two responses toward one who offends us—either we can forgive or we can become bitter. Bitterness,

53

I knew, has physical, mental, and spiritual consequences. Bitterness could cause me to become fatigued and depressed. It could cause numerous physical illnesses, and spiritually it could rob me of my relationship with God. I knew I could not afford to become bitter. But how could I forgive the same offense again and again and again?

Forgiveness means clearing another person's record with us, and transferring the responsibility for any punishment to God. I knew I needed the Lord's help with this one. Then I remembered Jesus' prayer when He needed to forgive. He prayed, "Father, forgive them; for they know not what they do." Why could Jesus do that? Simply because He viewed those who crucified Him as God's tools to carry out God's purpose for His life. Slowly I began to realize I must see my own dear husband as a tool God was using to develop a Christlike character in me. And as I forgive him, yes, again and again, that may give him a glimpse of Jesus and be the very thing that will draw him back to

God. I must also forgive so I can be forgiven; that is God's standard. I chose to forgive.

Chapter 13

He Comforteth Us

"Who comforteth us in all our tribulation" (II Corinthians 1:4).

If God is the Father of comfort and comforts us in all our tribulation, how does He do it? He has never spoken to me in an audible voice or come to me in a visible form. I am hurting, suffering, and weeping.

"God, You are the Father of comfort; why don't You do something for me? You say You love me; why don't You show me somehow? I need a visible sign."

Then the phone rang. It was a friend of mine who wanted to let me know she had not forgotten me and wanted to assure me she was still praying for me.

Suddenly I saw it. When God wants to do something for His children, He uses human instruments. He had brought me comfort through others so many times—through letters and cards and visits and gifts of food, money, and flowers. I came so close to missing what God was really doing for me because I failed to realize He does His work many times through fellow human beings.

God also comforts us through His Word. When I read God's promises and believe them, I am comforted. Believing is an act of the will. When I feel as if His promises are not true, I must will to believe them and repeat them over and over again until they sink into my mind.

God also comforts us by His Spirit. In John 14:16, the Spirit is called the Comforter, and we are told He abides with us.

When people come to bring us comfort, they leave again, but the Spirit remains with us. John 14:26 says, "But the Comforter, which is the Holy Ghost, whom the Father will send in my name, he shall teach you all things, and bring all things to your remembrance, whatsoever I have said unto you." The Spirit comforts us by bringing to our remembrance Scripture, songs, hymns, poems, and precious words of encouragement, just when we need it.

Just recently I experienced this so vividly. I was invited to a wedding, and the night before I was so tearful and fearful about facing the next day. The thought of a wedding just brought such a flood of feelings. And amid my tears and meditation, the following words of a song came to me:

"Grace enough, never mind
  tomorrow;
Grace enough, for every sorrow;
Grace enough, you need not borrow;
Ask of God, He'll see you through."

Why does God comfort us? God does not

comfort us merely to make us comfortable, but rather to make us comforters. God's comfort comes from Him to us, so it can go from us to someone else. We comfort others with words—with words such as, "I love you. I'll stand by you. I'm praying for you." We comfort others with deeds—making meals, baby-sitting, doing laundry, or taking someone shopping. We must be there. We must see the needs and offer to meet them. We can best comfort those who are experiencing a trial similar to a trial we have had. That doesn't mean, however, that we reach out to only those.

God wants all Christians involved in the ministry of comfort. Everyone needs comfort sometime in life. If you haven't needed it yet, rest assured you will. And everyone needs to give comfort sometime. If you haven't given comfort, the fact remains it was needed. I Thessalonians 5:11 is a command to all Christians: "Wherefore comfort yourselves together, and edify one another, even as also ye do."

Chapter 14

Acceptance

"Commit thy way unto the Lord; trust also in him; and he shall bring it to pass" (Psalm 37:5).

It has been said that acceptance spells peace. And many times I have read the motto, "God grant me the serenity to accept what I cannot change." But does that mean I must accept the fact that my husband is unfaithful to our marriage vows? Surely I cannot accept that. If I would accept that, he would never change, or so I thought.

Because I thought my situation was an exception, I did not accept it; and because I did not accept it, I did everything that I could possibly think of to change the situation myself. I tried crying, threatening, and being happy. I arranged for people to talk to him. I lavished him with love. I refused to love. I cooked feasts. I made soup. I gave him the silent treatment, I wrote him letters, I tried everything. But the situation did not change.

Finally, after many months, I think I have accepted that my husband is unfaithful to our marriage vows. I cannot change it, and I may as well get on with living. I have found that acceptance does spell peace—and joy, too. I believe God can change the situation, and I believe He will. But until then, by God's grace I am accepting the situation.

Chapter 15

Deliverance

"The angel of the Lord encampeth around about them that fear him, and delivereth them" (Psalm 34:7).

The Psalms became very precious to me during my time of testing. Many times I could identify with David as he cried out to God. One of his cries again and again was, "Lord, deliver me." That was the cry of my heart also. I wanted the Lord somehow to deliver me out of this difficult situation. After many months, I realized God did not see fit to deliver me. Slowly I began to see that deliverance may not mean out of a situation but rather to a place above it—that is, where I could experience joy and peace and victory even if the circumstances did not change one bit. So my prayer became, "Lord, please deliver me, if not 'out of,' then 'above' the situation." The Lord saw fit to answer this prayer.

I was thrilled when I learned in Hebrews 11 that though some heroes of faith were delivered out of a difficult situation, many others were instead given strength to remain faithful through suffering. In verses 33 and 34 we read of those who through faith obtained promises, stopped the mouths of lions, quenched the violence of fire, escaped the edge of the sword, and experienced other miraculous deliverances out of difficult situations. But in verses 35-38 we read, "Others were tortured, not accepting deliverance . . . others had trial of cruel mockings and scourging, yea, moreover of bonds and imprisonment: They were stoned . . . sawn asunder . . . tempted . . . slain with the sword: they wandered about in sheepskins and goatskins; being destitute, afflicted, tormented . . . they wandered in deserts, and in mountains, and in dens and caves of earth."

Then v. 39 spoke meaningfully to me, "And these all, having obtained a good report through faith, received not the promise." As I understand it, God wanted them to wait and share the even greater victory of those who do not experience deliverance out of a difficult situation but remain faithful through suffering until the end.

What God has done in the past, He is still able to do today. He, being God, has the right to do in my life that which brings the most glory to His name, and I must accept His deliverance whether it be "out of" or "above" a difficult situation. Either will be a victory.

Chapter 16

Patience

"Patient in tribulation" (Romans 12:12).

Patience is not a virtue I was born with, and now I find myself in God's "waiting room."

As I read James 1:4, I get the feeling that patience is a virtue that makes us almost perfect in God's sight: "But let patience have her perfect work, that ye may be perfect and entire, wanting nothing." Yet, when I read the Book of Job, and hear Job curse the day he was born, wonder why he had not died as a child, accuse God of ill-treatment, and complain of his plight, I wonder why he was considered patient.

What is patience? Is it never complaining or ever expressing your feelings? Is it gritting your teeth and saying, "If this is my lot, I will bear it"? How do we get patience? Are some temperaments fortunate enough to be born with it and others not? Does it become ours at the new birth, given by God in a neatly wrapped package?

No, no. I learned patience is the ability to bear with either adverse circumstances or difficult people without losing my faith in God. And it is developed day by day in the furnace of friction or affliction. Its results are cheerful acceptance of the divine work of God in one's life. Job's patience was expressed when he said, "Though he slay me, yet will I trust in him" (Job 13:15).

Chapter 17

Perseverance

"What, could ye not watch with me one hour?" (Matthew 26:40).

A friend of mine asked, "How long do we pray for your husband?" My heart sank. I could have asked, "Can you not watch with me one hour?"

Of all the mysteries of the prayer world the *why* of persevering prayer is one of the biggest. That our kind, loving heavenly Father must be supplicated day after day, or year after year is not easily understood. It is so easy for us to give up when our persevering supplications remain unanswered. For a time I struggled much over this mystery, but I have concluded that God has not told us why. He has only commanded us to persevere, and I need to obey.

In Luke 18:1-8, we have the parable of the unjust judge. In verse seven Jesus asks, "And shall not God avenge his own elect, which cry day and night unto him?" Crying day and night is surely a picture of persevering prayer. Then verse eight follows with the promise, "I tell you that he will avenge them speedily." The latter part of verse eight asks the question, "Nevertheless when the Son of man cometh, shall he find faith on the earth?"

Faith alone overcomes the difficulty of perseverance—faith that believes God is in control when circumstances make it look otherwise; faith that believes God has a right time and a right way wherein He will answer; faith that believes God is who He said He is, and that He will do everything His Word promises.

I told my friend I believe we need to pray for my husband until he repents or until he dies. Only God knows how long.

My own child asked me one day, "Mommy, why doesn't God answer our prayers?" I breathed a prayer for wisdom and said, "Just because God has not, does not say He will not. Maybe we will need to pray for twenty years." She replied, "I want God to answer now."

I became quite concerned about what would happen to my children's faith in God if God did not answer our prayers soon. Sometime later God gave me an illustration I shared with them. I said to them, "Suppose the pastor would ask for testimonies at church on Sunday morning. Suppose three persons would get up and testify of their deep love for God because He just answered a certain prayer that past week. Then suppose you would get up and say, 'I have been praying for Daddy every day for three years and God has not yet seen fit to answer my prayers, but I love the Lord and have faith in His power.' " I asked, "Which testimony would bring the most glory to God?" They got the point. I told them our faith in God has to go far beyond His answering our prayers. Our faith needs to be fixed upon God more because of who He is than because of what He does for us. I believe this truth in their hearts will cause their faith in God to remain.

I still do not know why I must persevere in prayer, but I have the promise that He will avenge His own elect that cry day and night unto Him.

"Faith is the substance of things hoped for, the evidence of things not seen" (Hebrews 11:1).

Chapter 18

Hope

"Hope we have as an anchor of the soul" (Hebrews 6:19).

I have one friend who keeps saying to me, "Things will not always be like they are now." That is hope.

Hope is very important to me or anyone who is suffering. Hope of getting well can carry us through an illness. Hope of having a healthy baby can carry us through a difficult delivery. Hope of a brighter future can carry us through a difficult today.

However, circumstances of life can loom so large, so permanent, and so dark that we can lose sight of hope. Then is when I need a friend to tell me, "Things will not always be like this."

The Christian has a ministry of hope. Hope is an anchor for the soul. Hope has sustained me through many a difficult day. A Christian's dearest hope, of course, is the hope of heaven. That is a hope we can always find comfort in and always hold out to other Christians.

My husband many times holds out hope by remarks such as, "We are going to make it. I cannot forget you. I am not happy this way. I love you all," or, "Pray for me." I find myself hanging on to each little thread of hope. Proverbs says, "Hope deferred maketh the heart sick" (13:12). I hang on to each thread of hope, as I said, but when hope is not acted upon, it is sickening. I need hope in order to face tomorrow. I am learning to place my hope in what God promises because that is the only hope that is sure and steadfast.

Chapter 19

Growth

"Giving all diligence, add to your faith" (II Peter 1:5).

Many of the books I have read indicate that God allows trials and affliction into our lives to produce growth. If this is true, I should be growing.

But what is growth? Our evangelist said, "Bible knowledge is not Christian growth; if it were, many of us would be spiritual giants."

Many great saints became great through severe trials. But others completely lost their faith in God when affliction came. This tells me it is not affliction that makes us but rather our response to it. We can rebel against or faint beneath or be exercised by affliction. How we respond will determine our growth.

If growth is not Bible knowledge, what is it? Growth, I learned, is measured by how much I depend upon God and how much the character of God is developed within me.

Little by little God has been removing the things in my life that brought security. At first I wanted to rebel. My lot seemed unfair. I compared myself with others and did not see bad things happening to them. But through my trials, my dependence upon God has slowly been growing.

As for God's character being developed in me, I feel others can see that better than I. God's supreme characteristic is His divine love. God places among us people who are difficult to love in order to develop His love in us. I would have many reasons to hate my husband, but I am challenged by the love that is described in I Corinthians 13. Divine love is patient, kind, never jealous, never proud, never selfish, does not demand its own way, is not touchy, does not hold grudges, will hardly notice when others do it wrong, is never glad about injustice, rejoices whenever truth wins out. If you love someone you will be loyal to him no matter what; you will believe in him, always expect the best of him, and stand your ground defending him.

I have to confess before God that I do not have this kind of love. When I confess, He forgives me and cleanses me and gives me His love. Then I can love the unlovely.

One writer stated that our rank in heaven will be determined by how much divine love has been developed in us.

The fruit of God's Spirit (the character of God) is not hung on us at the new birth. It is produced in our lives through various experiences, through Bible study and prayer, through sharing.

Christians are never finished growing. We are never fully mature Christians, but we should always be "maturing Christians."

Growth does not take place rapidly; it is a process. The process is sometimes painful.

Am I growing? God has given me an opportunity to grow. My growth depends upon my response to that opportunity.

Chapter 20

A Ministry

"Oh how love I thy law! it is my meditation all the day" (Psalm 119:97).

In times of affliction, we need something to take our minds off our own problems and nothing will be better than to minister in some way to others. For about five years I was a part of a small women's Bible study group. We gathered every Tuesday morning in an informal manner with only the Bible and one of the group as our teacher for the morning. It was a fellowship that meant a great deal to me. As time went on, it became my responsibility to teach the group on a regular basis. As I look back now, I realize God was providing for me through this responsibility the very thing that sustained me through a very trying time.

Psalm 119:92 says, "Unless thy law had been my delights, I should then have perished in mine affliction." This verse became a reality in my life. Many a night as I meditated on the Tuesday morning lesson and prepared it and gave it in my mind, I was kept from thinking thoughts that would have only caused turmoil. It was through disciplining my mind to meditate on God's Word and repeating over and over again to myself the great truths that God loves me, God cares about me, and God hears my prayers, that I learned to sleep when I did not know where my husband was, or did know and could have gone crazy thinking about it. The mind can think only one thought at a given time, and that is why

Isaiah 26:3 can be experienced. "Thou wilt keep him in perfect peace, whose mind is stayed on thee."

Every Christian should have a ministry. God can reveal to each of us where we fit into His ministering program. It is in giving of ourselves to others that we find fulfillment in life. Even Jesus said He "came not to be ministered unto, but to minister" (Matthew 20:28).

Chapter 21

God's Way

"For my thoughts are not your thoughts, neither are your ways my ways, saith the Lord" (Isaiah 55:8).

We have two darling daughters, ages eight and four, and I was quite excited to learn that the Lord was going to bless our home with another child. I truly believed my husband shared my excitement, but two months later my world caved in. My husband became distant, critical, uncommunicative. It was very obvious that his heart and mind were elsewhere. He was a long-distance truck driver, and the distances became longer and longer, and his coming-home times became less and shorter and more and more painful.

The remaining seven months were a nightmare. I could not eat or sleep and I cried much of the time. I could not understand God's timing for this baby. I did not want to bring a baby into a broken home. I feared for the well-being of our baby in light of the traumatic emotional upheaval in my life. All the books said a woman needs tender loving care at a time like this, and I was experiencing rejection and suffering like never before. The last long month the children and I were sick a lot. It was winter and we were having snowstorms. People were ministering to us in numberless ways.

Finally, on a Wednesday night, I went to the hospital via ambulance, on icy roads. My husband was not home, but the Lord met all my needs in a most marvelous way. After a quick delivery, the doctor announced I had a son. He was a healthy, normal, perfect baby. I was both thrilled and thankful.

Thursday morning I had a long-distance telephone call from my husband. He had called at home, and because no one answered, he called the hospital. I announced to him that he was daddy to his first son. It was difficult to detect his response on the phone. He was definitely overwhelmed with guilt for not being with me in a time of real need.

On Saturday he came to visit the baby and me. It was a most heartbreaking experience. I realized this was our baby and he seemed unable to respond or enter into the experience. His visit was short and extremely strained. I cried and wept with a broken heart all evening. I had hoped and prayed the baby would do something for him.

Sunday morning he brought Baby and me home. I experienced a tremendous mixture of joy and sorrow. I felt almost cruel taking a baby into the big, wide, wicked world. I felt alone with the responsibility of raising another child and was not sure I could handle it. He was a perfect baby. He ate and slept and grew. He brought tremendous joy into the lives of his sisters. He gave me a reason to live and a responsibility to meet.

Friends and relatives showered us with baby gifts and deeds of kindness. God was more real in this time of need than any other time. He gave me strength and grace abundantly.

Today I truly believe God is the blessed Controller of all things. I believe He timed perfectly the birth of our son. He has brought much joy to all who know him. He is friendly, happy, and healthy. I believe God has a special purpose for his life and will use him in building His kingdom. We named him Jason. His name means "healer." I believe he may be the instrument God will use to bring healing into our marriage.

"As for God his way is perfect" (II Samuel 22:31).

Chapter 22

Beware!

"Beware of false prophets, which come to you in sheep's clothing, but inwardly they are ravening wolves" (Matthew 7:15).

During my time of trial, I was faced with many decisions and at different stages needed counsel. I was shocked at the contradictory counsel of Christian people. One of the biggest decisions I had to make was how would I go about winning my husband back to God and myself. Some were sure that love was the answer—cook his favorite food, wash his clothes, do all the good deeds you can think of. Others said, "Do not put up with him—claim your rights, give him what he deserves." Then the most subtle line of all, "You can't take this."

Just the time I was convinced in my own mind that love was the answer, I would again hear the other side and be left in absolute confusion. One day I reached the limit and decided I must find God's answer. I spent one hour with a dear Christian lady who has an astounding knowledge of the Bible. After receiving some counseling, I spent the remainder of my time alone with God.

The first verse that God gave me was Proverbs 19:27: "Cease, my son, to hear the instruction that causeth to err from the words of knowledge." The Lord was telling me to stop listening to counsel that was not Scriptural. I know now I can no longer even listen to people who give me their own personal opinion apart from the Word of God.

Next the Lord gave me John 7:17. "If any man will do his will, he shall know. . . ." I knew in my heart I was willing to do God's will—whatever the cost—and was desperate to know.

Then the Lord showed me His purpose for suffering from the Book of I Peter. (I shared this in another chapter.) Until we see God's purpose for suffering, we will try any and every way to find an exit when we find ourselves in adverse circumstances.

Finally, the Lord gave me the following thoughts from Luke 6:27-38: "Love your enemies, do good to them which hate you, bless them that curse you, and pray for them which despitefully use you. . . . For if ye love them which love you, what thank have ye? . . . But love ye your enemies, and do good . . . hoping for nothing again; and your reward shall be great, and ye shall be the children of the Highest. . . . Forgive, and ye shall be forgiven: Give and it shall be given unto you." God was telling me to love—do good, pray, bless, forgive. Nowhere could I find God saying, "Lock him out. Claim your rights. Give him what he deserves."

I don't know what the reward will be or just what it means to be the "children of the Highest," but reading these verses, I became excited.

Suddenly I knew what my response was to be toward my husband, but somehow it didn't matter whether I would win him or not. I saw that this way I would have God's approval and blessing, and that was all that mattered.

I Peter 3:9 says, "Not rendering evil for evil, or railing for railing: but contrariwise blessing; knowing that ye are thereunto called, that ye should inherit a blessing." God was telling me to return evil with a blessing and that in turn I would inherit a blessing.

Romans 12:20: "Therefore if thine enemy hunger, feed him; if he thirst, give him drink: for in so doing thou shalt heap coals of fire on his head." The study helps in my Dake's Bible said that heaping coals of fire on an enemy's head will bring him a burning sense of shame. True shame is among the first elements of true repentance.

Proverbs 20:22: "Say not thou, I will recompense evil; but wait on the Lord, and he shall save thee." Vengeance is not my responsibility: that is God's business. Nowhere in the Bible can I find it my duty to give my husband what he may deserve.

I am disappointed with Christians who give their own personal feelings and opinions as counsel. The Bible has the only answer that is right and dependable. If we cannot find the answer ourselves because of limited knowledge, we need to go to somone who can help us. But we must beware! Not everyone who is a Christian, not everyone who calls himself a counselor, is capable of giving us God's Word in the matter.

Chapter 23

I Will Be a Father

"A father of the fatherless" (Psalm 68:5).

What a revelation! I do not need to be a father and a mother to my children. God Himself will be a father to them. I pray, "Oh Lord, give me wisdom and strength to be the very best mother. Show me how to meet the emotional and spiritual needs of my children. Aid me in providing for them all the love and security they need to grow up emotionally stable. And thank You, thank You for being a father to them."

Line upon line and precept upon precept I endeavored to teach my children that God is a father to them. I told them over and over, "God loves you. He is with you always, and He will never forsake you. He puts you under His wing just as a chicken does her baby chicks." Then one night I heard my daughter pray, "Thank You, God, for being a father to me." It was like being rewarded; she got the message!

God has been faithful to His promise. A lot of His being a father has been done through a grandfather or an uncle or a friend. I have the confidence my children will not grow up marred and scarred in spite of circumstances, because God is the very best father a child could have.

Chapter 24

Thy Maker Is Thy Husband

"Thy Maker is thine husband; the Lord of hosts is his name" (Isaiah 54:5).

I was thoroughly enjoying our week of revival meetings. I really needed the truths I was grasping. But Friday night came and the sermon was on husband-wife relationships. My heart sank and I questioned whether I should not have stayed at home. The minister explained in detail the wife's responsibility. She is to submit to her husband, rely upon him, and need him. He reminded husbands of their responsibility to love, protect, and provide for their wives.

When I got home, I said, "Well, Lord, what shall I do with that message? I would love to apply it but I can't; my husband is not even here." Gently He reminded me, "Aren't you claiming your Maker as your husband?" I thought, "Yes, Lord." Then He showed me that He wants me to submit to Him and rely on Him and need Him and that He wants to love me, protect me, provide for me. It was such a marvelous revelation. It caused me to rejoice.

Chapter 25

Miserable Comforters

"Lord, all my desire is before thee; and my groaning is not hid from thee" (Psalm 38:9).

One day one of my "friends" came to me insisting, "It takes two to make a marriage and two to break a marriage." I was already crushed and this only dealt another death blow. I could see that it takes two to make a marriage, but I was quite sure one could break it.

Time and again I asked my husband to share with me where I had failed. But he never said anything specific; rather, that it was not my failure. I was a good housekeeper, cook, and seamstress. I thought I was a good wife and mother. Comparing myself with what I saw in other women, I considered myself at least average or normal. I could not grasp where I had failed as a wife, but in the back of my mind I had the nagging thought that he must be finding something elsewhere that he did not find in me. I prayed and prayed that God would show me where I failed. I felt it very essential for me to know so that, should we be reconciled, I would not make the same error again.

When God knew I could accept it and respond to it, He gently showed me I had failed my husband on the emotional level. I found I was very ignorant of what a man's emotional needs are. But God was teaching me. It was extremely painful to have my eyes opened to my failures as a wife, and I wanted to condemn myself, hate myself, and call myself a failure and give up. But I chose to confess my failure to God, man, and my husband, believing God then would give me the grace to keep on and change as I continued to humble myself.

Chapter 26

Lord, Change Me

"He which hath begun a good work in you will [continue to] perform it" (Philippians 1:6).

After God showed me some of my failures as a wife, my prayer became, "Lord, change me. Develop in me 'even the ornament of a meek and quiet spirit, which is in the sight of God of great price' " (I Peter 3:4).

I knew I had to change. I knew the

change had to be in my spirit and attitude, not just putting on a right action.

What brings about change in one's life? Is it a result of praying, "Lord, change me"? Is it a self-effort, or is it purely the work of God? Is change instantaneous or does it come about gradually? These were the questions I asked myself and others.

As much as I wished I could change myself overnight, I recognized it to be the work of God which takes place gradually as I learn to cooperate with Him. God's part is changing; my part is cooperating.

Chapter 27

Waiting on the Lord

"Wait on the Lord: be of good courage, and he shall strengthen thine heart: wait, I say, on the Lord" (Psalm 27:14).

Some time ago I was seated in the waiting room of a doctor's office. The room was crowded and the doctor seemed to be behind schedule. It was interesting to watch those who were waiting. Some were reading; some were doing nothing; some enjoyed visiting. One man came in and surveyed the roomful of people and went directly to the receptionist's desk and asked, "How long will I have to wait?" I could not hear her reply, but he stalked out of the office grumbling, "I will come back later."

Since the beginning of time, many saints have found themselves in God's waiting room. Over and over again the Word tells us to "wait on the Lord." What is our response when this is God's word to us? Are we occupied with something else while we wait, as those were who were reading in the doctor's office? Or do we sit doing nothing—letting out an impatient sigh occasionally? Or are we like the man who stalked out of the room—impatient and certainly not willing to waste time waiting?

I for one do not like to wait on man or God. When I was a child, we did not have a car, and when we wanted to go away, we sometimes had to hire a taxi. I still remember staring at the clock and waiting impatiently for the driver, who always seemed to be late. How I hated that waiting!

Presently I am occupied in a project that cannot proceed until another person involved is ready to move ahead. Only yesterday I discussed it with him and he said, "Keep working on it; we will just wait awhile to proceed further." He gave no explanation as to the reason for waiting. Sometimes I have felt the only word God seems able to speak is *wait*.

Several weeks ago I became quite desperate concerning my husband's delayed repentance. I really thought the time may be ripe, but nothing happened. In my desperation I decided to spend a day fasting, praying, and reading the Bible. I asked God to show me if anything in my life might be hindering His working out my husband's repentance. The Lord did not show me anything new. His answer once again seemed simply to be "WAIT."

I have heard all the cute sayings such as, "God doesn't reckon time as we do. God is never in a hurry, but always on time. God's time may not be our time." But really, why does God require us to wait? What is time spent in God's waiting room meant to teach us? What should our response be while waiting? I set out to find answers.

Genesis 21:2 says, "For Sarah conceived, and bare Abraham a son in his old age, at the set time of which God had spoken to him." This verse bears out that God has a set time to do things. Some things cannot be done in a day; then we must wait. Abraham had to wait many years for the promised son. God did not tell him the number of years he would need to wait. Neither does He tell us. If He did, perhaps we would faint! However, when we are waiting on God, we will not be disappointed. Delays are not necessarily denials. There are secrets of love and wisdom we do not understand in God's delays. We would like to pluck God's mercies green when God would have them to be ripe.

Waiting is twofold. It may be us waiting on God, or it may be God waiting on us.

Mary and Martha had to wait on God

when Lazarus died. Jesus did not come until Lazarus was dead four days. God's purpose in making them wait was to bring forth more glory, to do more than their expectations. He did not want merely to heal Lazarus; He wanted to raise him from the dead.

Moses had to wait forty years to be used of God to deliver the Israelites out of Egypt. But really God was waiting until Moses was spiritually ready to be used. Forty years earlier, Moses had tried to deliver them in his own strength. God waited to send Moses until He knew Moses would depend on Him.

Waiting is much more difficult than being active. Waiting requires patience, and patience is a rare virtue. Psalm 37:7 tells us how to wait: "Rest in the Lord, and wait patiently for Him." Patience removes worry and self-effort. With patience we can rest in the Lord while we wait.

Like Abraham, we may be long tried, but through patient endurance, we will receive the promise.

Chapter 28

Frustrations

"If any of you lack wisdom, let him ask of God" (James 1:5).

I was attending a seminar. About the third session I became frustrated. Either I was an exception to some of the principles being taught, or there was no hope for my family.

I was depressed over statements such as:

"A child forms his concept of God through his earthly father."

"A girl who does not have a warm, loving, close relationship with her father will have all kinds of problems when dating."

"When a husband does not assume leadership in the home—particularly spiritual leadership with discipline of the children—and the wife then assumes the responsibility, it will not work."

I shared my frustrations with a few of my friends and then came home and earnestly prayed that God would help me discover His answers for me.

The statement that a child's concept of God is formed by the father was not new to me; but I decided to take more definite action in regard to understanding it, and I asked God to direct me. My children's father is too busy to be a father. He has forsaken them. He has hurt them. God is not like that, and I desperately wanted to convey this to them. I began by telling them that our speaker said, "Children think God is like their daddy, but God is not like your daddy. God is never too busy to pay attention to us. God will never forsake us. God loves us very dearly."

Then I took my Bible and picked out verses that speak about the character of God, and with a black marking pencil, I wrote them in large letters on a sheet of paper and put them on our refrigerator. I told them we would read these verses every day. I went to all ends to explain the meaning of the words describing God—words and phrases such as *merciful, full of compassion, plenteous in mercy, good to all, nigh unto the broken-hearted.* Then I told them we are going to have a theme song in our home and it would be: "God is so good; God is so good; God is so good; He's so good to me." We would add verses of our own such as: "God is so kind, God cares for us, God answers prayer," etc.

Daily I began taking my two-year-old into my arms and telling him, "God loves you, Son. He is so kind. He is so good to us. He is watching over you. He cares about us and He sees everything we do."

I decided it was my responsibility to form their concept of God, and this is how

I set out to do it.

My children cannot have an ideal relationship with their daddy when he is seldom with them, so I am desperate that they develop a meaningful relationship with God. I put forth some new efforts in our prayer time together. I began by telling them when we pray we do not only want to ask God for things and thank God for things, but also want to just talk to Him and tell Him how we feel. I began pouring out more of my feelings to God in my prayers with them to show them how to do the same. I believe this is a key to developing a warm, close, loving relationship with God, and I pray it will compensate for their father's absence. Hopefully, this should eliminate the problem our speaker said they would have in their relationships during their teenage years.

As for assuming leadership in the home, I consider my situation different from that where a husband is home. When a husband is present, it is definitely his responsibility; when he is absent, it becomes his wife's.

I believe there is hope for my family. My confidence is based on a decision I made when I was fifteen. Then I invited Jesus Christ into my heart and life. I confessed to God that I was a sinner, and I placed my faith in Jesus, the One who died on the cross for my sins. Now I can experience forgiveness and become a part of God's family. There is also hope for my children as they place their faith in Jesus. Being a child of God allows me to claim the promises in His Word.

One of the very precious promises to me is found in Psalm 103:17, 18: "But the mercy of the Lord is from everlasting to everlasting upon them that fear him, and his righteousness unto children's children; to such as keep his covenant, and to those that remember his commandments to do them." To me this is saying if I reverence God and obey Him, His mercy is upon me and my children. Best of all, from everlasting to everlasting—not just today and maybe tomorrow. These promises are mine to claim because I am His. These promises give me hope for my family!

Chapter 29

Loneliness

"Lo, I am with you alway" (Matthew 28:20).

Aloneness need not be loneliness when one has Jesus. One day I found myself singing, "Jesus Christ Is All I Need." From my very inner being, I felt His presence with me. He was real to me. He was my companion. I talked to Him when I went to bed until I went to sleep, and it was personal and satisfying. I talked to

Him the first thing in the morning and all through the day. He really was Wonderful . . . Counselor . . . Mighty God . . . Everlasting Father . . . Prince of Peace. I thought I had arrived that day when I sang so honestly, "Jesus Christ Is All I Need." But then one day He seemed to say to me, "You say I am all you need; now I want to become all you want." I thought, "Oh, no, Lord, You are asking too much of me. You are not asking this of other people. My friends may have their husbands and I will always want mine, too. Surely that is only fair. Lord, why do You ask so much of me? Aren't You ever satisfied?" Then I thought of Psalm 23:1, "The Lord is my Shepherd; I shall not want." To me it was saying, "The Lord is my Shepherd; that is all I want." I am still struggling with this one, but I want to be satisfied with Jesus.

Holidays can be very painful for someone who is alone. I learned I needed to plan ahead for those days so my aloneness would not cause me loneliness. I learned to invite people rather than hoping to be invited. I learned to celebrate for the sake of my children in spite of the fact that my husband would not be with us. When I am creative in my planning, God often provides an extra blessing or surprise by an unexpected invitation or welcome visitors.

Books, too, are my friends, and with a good book many an otherwise lonely evening has quickly passed by. Hobbies, tapes, and records can fill many otherwise lonely hours.

Preventing loneliness means disciplining the mind. I have found that after I have the children in bed for the night and have a few hours alone, it is no time to think about my friends, who say they sit at the table and have coffee after the children are in bed and share the day's events. If I must talk to someone, that is a good time to call another "alone friend."

Again I say, aloneness need not be loneliness if we have Jesus. He "is a friend that sticketh closer than a brother" (Proverbs 18:24).

Chapter 30

Who Am I?

"I have formed thee; thou art my servant" (Isaiah 44:21).

I am not divorced. I am not a widow. And I am not single. But I do not really have a husband. Where do I fit? I cannot go out with the single girls because I have children to take care of. I do not fit in with the widows. The few I do know are much older. And I do not fit with the married couples because I am without a husband. This can be a very painful realization. At times it almost causes me to withdraw from socializing. Weekdays are not so bad; I can move around in a woman's world. Weekends can be painful. I could identify with my child when she said, "Mommy, I hate to walk into church because everyone has a daddy to walk with but me."

I enjoy entertaining, but it is awkward to have families when my husband is not here to visit with the men, say grace at the table, and help with the children. Picnics and reunions are terrible. Helping three children fill paper plates with food, get drinks, and find a place to sit is no cinch. Then when my plate is filled, I realize all the other couples are sitting as families and I have no one to sit with. Sometimes I weigh the hurt of being home alone, and choose what I feel gives the least pain. We are a couple-oriented society, and it hurts to move about alone.

There have been painfully awkward moments, but God has been very gracious in giving me a very wonderful, thoughtful, considerate, kind, and helpful church family as well as many friends who have done extremely much to make a difficult road smooth.

These hurts are temporary. I know I shall fit perfectly somewhere in God's eternal kingdom. "Until then, with joy I'll carry on!"

Chapter 31

Suffering

"Wherefore let them that suffer according to the will of God commit the keeping of their souls to him in well doing, as unto a faithful Creator" (I Peter 4:19).

When I read the above verse, I was taken aback with the phrase, "suffer according to the will of God." Could suffering really be God's will for me?

Being human, I shy away from suffering. I do not want it. Even Jesus prayed,

"Let this cup pass from me; nevertheless not as I will, but as thou wilt" (Matthew 26:39). I believe the suffering was what made Him ask God to remove the cup.

I asked myself, "Why would God will suffering upon one of His children?" Psalm 4:1 says, "Thou hast enlarged me when I was in distress." *Enlarged* means "prepared for the task ahead." Sometimes God brings suffering into our lives to prepare us for some future work. My present distress may enable me to minister effectively to others who are suffering a similar circumstance.

Psalm 119:71 says, "It is good for me that I have been afflicted; that I might learn thy statutes." Through my suffering, God's Word has become very precious to me. I read it groping for some word of comfort or guidance. Because God has comforted me through His Word, I endeavor to comfort others with this same comfort.

Job 23:10b says, "When he hath tried me, I shall come forth as gold." God uses suffering to purify our lives. Gold is put into a furnace of fire, not to destroy the gold, but only to consume the dross! Self-righteousness, materialism, prayerlessness, carnality, jealousy, gossip, anger, and many more such things are dross in our lives that God wants to consume. He does not put us into the furnace of affliction to destroy us but only to purge these impurities from our lives.

Lamentations 3:32, 33 says, "But though he cause grief, yet will he have compassion according to the multitude of his mercies. For he doth not afflict willingly." Suffering is not necessarily God punishing us. God is a God of love, not someone who thinks of cruel ways to make us suffer. He wants to use suffering to bring about greater Christlikeness in us. Much of the suffering we experience is due to human selfishness and sin. God does not will the evil of sin, but He does permit it. God takes the unpleasant circumstances of the life of one who loves Him and works it together for good.

In Isaiah 43:2, God says, "When thou passest through the waters, I will be with thee." This is God's promise, but God never promised the Christian that his life would be easy; neither does He give us an explanation for everything He allows. However, He has promised to be with us through it all.

Suffering produces compassion. It makes us alert to the hidden hurts of another. As we become involved in the sufferings of another, cords of love develop between us and bind us together. People acquainted with suffering seldom give quick, pat answers; but rather acquire the gift of comforting others. In this way God uses our suffering for His glory.

Suffering is ours for just a little while that we may gain eternal glory. When life is over, suffering will be taken away and everlasting joy will be God's gift to His children. "Hallelujah! What a Saviour!"

Chapter 32

Fulfillment

"I am come that they might have life, and that they might have it more abundantly" (John 10:10).

I believe God has planned a life that brings fulfillment for each of us regardless of our age, education, or marital status. But what is it that brings fulfillment?

One man testified that he has a beautiful wife whom he loves dearly; he has wholesome, alert, fine children; the business endeavors in which he invested himself are successful; he has gained financial independence and security. Every aim and ambition he had set for himself as a young man have been achieved and even surpassed, but at age forty he was acutely aware that there was something significant lacking. He was not experiencing fulfillment? What was wrong?

After my marriage fell apart, I found myself discovering what brings fulfillment. Previously I had experienced a lot of satisfaction through meeting my husband's needs. I enjoyed cooking for him. I made clothes for him. I ran errands for him. I loved him, and much of my life revolved around him. Gradually all of this stopped. I had to find satisfaction and fulfillment some other way. The above testimony sharply reminded me it is not found in things or success or even a good marriage relationship. *Where is it?* and *How is it found?* were my questions.

I was reminded of the Scripture that says, "He that loseth his life for my sake shall find it" (Matthew 10:39). To me that was the key. Losing my life meant saying, "Lord, here I am. Take me and do with me whatever You want."

When we have that attitude, God can and will work in us and through us, and that is a fulfilled life. Many people are trying to find fulfillment by catering to self. Their whole life revolves around themselves and getting what they want and doing what they please, but they are left empty on the inside.

Today my greatest fulfillment is found in the things that God is doing through me. And God can work through me in spite of my marital status. He can work through anyone who will sincerely say, "Here I am, Lord; do in me and through me whatever You want to do."

Chapter 33

Needs

"But my God shall supply all your need according to his riches in glory by Christ Jesus" (Philippians 4:19).

Through all of this, my husband has amply met all my financial needs, and I appreciate this very much. With a family to care for, it would be very difficult if I had to go out and work, and it would be humiliating to have to depend on others. We do need food, clothes, and shelter, and

I thank the Lord and my husband for providing our monetary needs.

However, God having created mankind with a body, soul, and a spirit, I have emotional and spiritual needs as well as physical needs.

I have the emotional need for love, security, appreciation, acceptance, significance, etc., and my husband certainly has not been meeting these needs.

As I was meditating on the above verse of Scripture, the words "all your need" stood out. I decided to claim this verse for my emotional needs as well. I know many other people have claimed it for physical or financial needs. When my heart longs for love and security and appreciation and acceptance, I cry out to God in prayer, saying, "Lord, You made me. You placed within me these emotional needs. You know what I feel. You know how I hurt. And You promised to meet all my need according to Your riches in glory by Christ Jesus; therefore, I am coming to You. These needs I am feeling have driven many a woman like myself to another

123

man, to pleasure-seeking or drugs or alcohol or overeating, and I know I cannot go that road; therefore, I am coming to You." Then I visualize the presence of Jesus and commune with Him. I do not have ecstatic feelings; yet, time and time again my needs are met.

I think a woman's spiritual needs involve having someone with whom to share new insights from God's Word, or questions about God's Word, and someone to share prayer burdens and joy. I always loved to hear my husband pray. I loved to see him kneel by his living-room chair in prayer before he left for work. When I saw him lean on God, I felt so able to lean on him. I loved holding hands at the doorway each Sunday morning as he led us in prayer before going to church.

But the Lord has been faithful in meeting my spiritual needs also. I have a certain number of friends with whom I can share my prayer burdens. I have enjoyed rich times of sharing on a spiritual level with several dear friends from church.

God has placed me under His umbrella and there my needs are met! Yes, *all* my needs according to His riches in glory, and His is no meager supply.

Chapter 34

Yielding Rights

"Blessed are the meek: for they shall inherit the earth" (Matthew 5:5).

When my husband mentioned getting a divorce, I was grief-stricken. My first response was one of revenge. I told him that if this was the route he wanted to take, he would be the greater loser. I told him that the children would be mine, and he would see them only when he had visitation rights, and I would limit them as much as I possibly could. I told him that this house would be our home and not his, and he would then enter only as a visitor. I reminded him that it would be his responsibility to support the children, and I would see to it that he did. I knew in light of his life the law would be in my favor.

Time went on and he did not file for a divorce because he did not want to lose his children, but neither did our relationship improve.

One night it seemed as though I could not endure any more trying circumstances, and I cried out to God in desperation asking for direction. The Lord seemed to be telling me to give up everything, even my children. I struggled a long time before I was willing to do this, but finally the victory was won. The next time my husband called we had a long talk. I told him, "I sense you are not getting a divorce because of what I said about the children. However, you are not working on rebuilding our marriage either, so I have changed my mind." I said,

"Go ahead and get the divorce if that is what you want. I will work with you about seeing the children. I ask only two things of you—do not come here with your friend, and do not take the children away from here. Anytime you want to spend time with them, you may come, and then I will go shopping or something. I am sure I shall need a break once in a while and that would be a perfect time."

I then explained to him my former reasons for not wanting him to see the children. I had felt since he was not a Christian, he might undo the teaching I was giving them; and also, if he did not love me, he might try to turn them against me. But I told him I decided they are his children as much as mine and if those things happened, the responsibility would be on him.

I felt as though I had given up everything I held dear and was most amazed to hear him say, "I do not really want a divorce, and I would never try to undo the way you teach the children." It seemed as though what he was asking for he did not really want.

I call this yielding my rights . . . giving up what I feel is mine by right. When I do this, I know God will give them back to me if He wants me to have them. I have been able to give up my rights only as I have trusted God and remembered that He is in control.

Chapter 35

Hurts

"He healeth the broken in heart, and bindeth up their wounds" (Psalm 147:3).

One day I wrote in my journal, "I hurt terrible inside." What was I to do with my deep inner hurt? Was I to hurt the rest of my life? What was the answer? I knew the answer was not suppressing my feelings, neither was it trying to explain my hurts to everyone who would listen, so I wept and prayed, saying, "Lord, You said

You would bind up the broken-hearted and heal their wounds. Why don't You do it for me?"

One evening I met a lady who had experienced a multitude of hurts, many more than my own, and she told me she does not hurt anymore. I questioned the truth of her statement, but also decided that if she could come through so much and not hurt, there must be a way for me also.

I reread Catherine Marshall's book, *To Live Again*. She shared that after Peter's death, she was told a change of setting would hasten the healing process. She said for her that would have been running away. Neither was that my answer. My children and I needed the security that home, church, and friends were providing. She also said broken hearts need work to do. There is therapy in the necessary mechanics. This I found to be very true. I needed a job. As a mother of three, I had one. I needed a ministry. I had to reach outside my four walls, and the Lord gave me opportunities. I needed a hobby—I had several, mainly sewing. Frustrations melted away as I pushed the pedal of my sewing machine many hours.

Marshall confirmed in my mind that hiding the emotions was not the answer. Forcing one's self to be brave will not heal the hurt. There is much release in letting the tears flow. Here I had to find a balance. Around most people I did force myself to appear brave, but there were always a chosen few with whom I could let the tears flow and experience a real release.

There is therapy in opening wide one's heart to other people. We need to accept as fully as we can the love that flows from friends and family. The one who shuts his heart on people is shutting his heart on God, because God uses human instruments to do His work. However, it is God alone who can finally heal the broken-hearted. Christ alone is the physician for the spirit.

Catherine Marshall said one afternoon she met an elderly, gray-haired lady. To her she poured out all her hurts, feelings, and fears. The lady listened, speaking very little, shedding a few tears now and then. Then when she was done speaking, the lady said, "I have only one remedy for what ails you. Let's talk to Christ about it." Her prayer was a simple heartfelt claiming of Christ's promise to heal the broken-hearted. Catherine said, "From that moment, healing began. This specific asking for the touch of the great Physician was an invaluable step. It was effective because it was personally for me in my presence."

The lady I met who had had a multitude of hurts did something very similar to that for me. A real healing began in my life also as a result. The question in my mind was, Why didn't someone pray that prayer with me several years sooner? This is a responsibility Christians need to assume for the hurting, we fail them if we do not. It is not just a casual prayer made when you think of a hurting person. It is a specific prayer, with the person who is sorrowing, out of sincere caring, for God to heal the broken heart.

Could this be what Galatians 6:2 means? "Bear ye one another's burdens, and so fulfil the law of Christ."

I thank God for the healing He has wrought in my experience. However, it does not mean I never hurt. I compare it to the hurt of a broken arm or leg. The wound has healed, but sometimes weather conditions cause it to hurt for a day or so even many years later. My wound has healed, but there are occasions when I hurt deeply for a day or so.

Chapter 36

Joy

"My brethren, count it all joy when you fall into divers temptations" (James 1:2).

I prayed, "Lord, can I be happy in all of this? Can I experience joy now?"

I picked up my Bible and turning to the Psalms, read, "Wait on the Lord: be of good courage, and he shall strengthen thine heart" (Psalm 27:14). There was my answer. Surely being of good courage did not mean walking around with a sad face.

I studied the Spirit fruit called joy and learned it is not dependent upon circumstances, but rather it is the result of a relationship with Jesus Christ. The source of joy is Jesus. Knowing my sins are forgiven, walking in daily fellowship with Jesus, accepting His plan for my life, knowing I will spend eternity in heaven if I remain faithful to God—all this gives me joy that no circumstance of life can alter.

Happiness is momentary and fleeting. It can be here today and gone tomorrow, depending on circumstances.

Philippians 4:4 says, "Rejoice in the Lord alway: and again I say, Rejoice." Our circumstances may not give us much to rejoice about, but we can always rejoice in the Lord. He loves us. He died for us. He cares about every detail of our lives. He will never fail us or forsake us.

I have come to realize that long ago with the trials God allows in our lives, He also sends blessings. There are many little joys scattered throughout my life. What a joy to have my little son burst into the sewing room and say spontaneously, "Oh, I love you, my dear mommy." What a joy to wake up in the morning without an ache or a pain. What a joy to attend teacher conferences and hear that your child is doing exceptionally well in school. What a joy to have your secret sister send you fresh strawberry pie. What a joy to get an unexpected letter in the mail. What a joy to open God's Word and find just the promise you were needing. Within every day is hidden something to enjoy the little joys that are along the way. The choice is ours.

Chapter 37

In the Midst of the Valley

"I will open . . . fountains in the midst of the valleys" (Isaiah 41:18).

My story is not a fairy tale. It does not end, "And they lived happily ever after." The last of my journal is not yet written. If it were, I do not know what it would say. I am still in the midst of the valley.

I do not know how God will deal with my husband in the future. I can only share what He has done, and is doing, in my life. I am still journeying on. The road has not been smooth, but God's grace has been sufficient. There are fountains in the midst of the valley.

My husband has filed for a divorce recently, but he has told his lawyer to hold it because he does not want to proceed with it. To me it does not make sense. It is like a threat hanging over my head. But I have committed it to God. My times are in His hands.

More recently I found a note pinned on a gift left in my bedroom. It said: "To my dear wife. I love you. We are going to work things out. I want to give you and our children all my love."

It is a thread of hope I am hanging on to.

I have personalized II Corinthians 4:8, 9, and 18; it is my personal testimoney:

"[I] am troubled on every side, yet not distressed; [I] am perplexed, but not in despair; persecuted, but not forsaken; cast down, but not destroyed; while [I] look not at the things which are seen, but at the things which are not seen: for the things which are seen are temporal; but the things which are not seen are eternal."

Praise the Lord, the best is yet to come!

Epilogue

I wanted to end my story with a miracle. I wanted the miracle to be a prodigal returned to God and his family. But it is not so. A no-fault divorce was filed in Berks County court in July, 1982, five years after it all began. I came before God in helplessness, pleading my case. Divorce was not my plan. I believe in marriage as a commitment until death. But because God has allowed it, I will accept it, because He has promised that all things work together for good to those that love Him. "All things" must include the divorce. I do not know what God has in store for my future, but I know He will not fail me. His thoughts toward me are thoughts of peace and not of evil.

However, there is also a miracle. The miracle is God's all-sufficient grace in my life and the lives of my children. It is holding us together, close to Him. He has promised His grace, and His mercies are new every morning. The words of the following song express my feeling:

Because He lives, I can face tomor-
      row,
Because He lives, all fear is gone;
Because I know He holds the future,
And life is worth the living just be-
      cause He lives.
     —Gloria and William Gaither